Dear *Grandma*

from you to me®

Dear *Grandma*
from you to me®

This book is for your Grandmother's unique and amazing story.

It is for her to capture some of her life's key memories, experiences and feelings.

Ask her to complete it carefully and, if she wants to, add some photographs or images to personalise it more.

When it is finished and returned to you, this will be a record of her story . . . a story that you will treasure forever.

Dear

Here is my letter to you ...

Tell me about the time and place you were born . . .

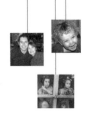

What are your earliest memories?

I'd like to know about your parents . . . names, dates of birth and tell me some stories about them . . .

Tell me what you know about your Mother's parents and family . . .

Tell me what you know about your Father's parents and family . . .

Please detail what you know of our family tree . . .

What **interesting** information do you know about other people in our family?

Here's some space for you to add more about our family that will **interest** generations to come . . .

What do you remember about the place/s you lived when you were a child?

What were your favourite childhood toys or games?

What sort of pets did you have when you were young and what were their names?

What do you remember about your holidays as a child?

What did you do for **entertainment** when you were young?

What did you **study** at school and what were you **best** at?

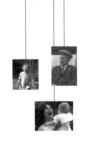

Tell me about the things you did as a child that are different for today's children . . .

What did you want to do when you grew up?

What were your favourite hobbies when you were young?

Did you have an idol when you were young?
Tell me who and why . . .

What was the first piece of music you bought?

What chores had to be done when you were young that aren't needed to be done today?

Describe any **family traditions** you had or maybe still have . . .

What age were you when you started work?
Tell me about the jobs you have had . . .

How did you meet my Grandfather?

What would you do for a night-out when you were dating?

Tell me about a **special** piece of **music** that you and my Grandfather had 'just for you' ...

Describe your wedding . . .

Choosing the names for your children can be really difficult . . . how did you decide?

I would love to know more about my parents
. . . what can you tell me?

Tell me what my **Mum** / **Dad** was **like** when they were younger . . .

How did you feel when you were told you were going to be a grandparent?

What did you think when you first saw me after
I was born?

Can you see any characteristics in me that come from other people in our family?

j

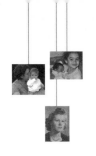

In what ways am I similar or different to my Mum / Dad?

Describe some of your favourite memories of the times we have spent together ...

Describe what you **like** about me . . .

Is there anything you would like to change about me?

Tell me about the friends you have had in your life . . .

What piece/s of music would you choose in your own favourite 'top 10'?

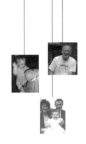

Tell me about the **furthest** place you have **travelled** to . . .

What are the happiest or greatest memories
of your life?

What are a few of your favourite things?

Describe your memory of some major world events that have happened in your lifetime . . .

Describe the greatest change that you have seen in your lifetime so far . . .

Do you think life today is better or worse than when you were young? How is it different?

Who or what has been the greatest influence on you?

If you were an **animal** . . . what **type** of animal would you be, and why?

If you won the Lottery . . . what would you do with the money?

What have you found most difficult in your life?

What is your **biggest regret** in your life?

Can you do anything about it **now**?

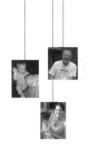

Tell me about the things that have made you happy or laugh ...

With hindsight what would you do **differently**?

Describe something you still want to achieve in your life . . .

Tell me something you think I won't know about you . . .

What would you like your epitaph to say?

Given your experiences, what advice would you like to offer me?

And now your chance to tell me some other **personal stories** that you want to share . . .

These extra pages are for us to write any **questions, memories** or **answers** that may not have been covered elsewhere in the book . . .

And finally for the record . . .

what is your full name ?

what was your maiden name ?

what is your date of birth ?

what colour are your eyes ?

how tall are you ?

what blood group are you ?

what was the date when you completed this story for me ?

*And a few words to thank you for
completing this Journal of a Lifetime ...*

If you liked the concept of this book, please tell your family and friends and look out for others in the current from you to me range.

Journals of a Lifetime
Dear Mum
Dear Dad
Dear Grandad
Dear Daughter
Dear Son
Dear Sister
Dear Brother
Dear Friend

Home Gift Journals
Cooking up Memories
Digging up Memories

You can also use this code by downloading a free QR code reader app to your smart phone.

Sport Gift Journals
Kicking off Memories
Try to Remember

Personal Development Journals
Dear Future Me

Leaving Gift Journals
These were the Days
Primary School Journals

Parent & Baby
Mum to Mum ... pass it on
Bump to first Birthday ... pregnancy & first year journal
Our Story ... for my Daughter
Our Story ... for my Son

Christmas Memories
Christmas Past, Christmas Present

Personalised
You can personalise your own Journal of a Lifetime online at www.fromyoutome.com

All titles are available at gift and book shops or online at www.fromyoutome.com

Dear Grandma

from you to me®

First published in the UK by *from you to me*, August 2007
Copyright, *from you to me* limited 2007
Hackless House, Murhill, Bath, BA2 7FH
www.fromyoutome.com
E-mail: hello@fromyoutome.com

ISBN 978-1-907048-02-9

Cover design by so design consultants, Wick, Bristol, UK   www.so-design.co.uk
Printed and bound in the UK by CPI Group (UK) Ltd, Croydon, CR0 4YY

This paper is manufactured from material sourced from forests certified according to strict environmental, social and economical standards.

MIX
Paper from
responsible sources
FSC® C013604

If you think other questions should be included in future editions, please let us know. And please share some of the interesting answers you receive with us at the from you to me website to let other people read about these fascinating insights . . .